MICROWAVE COOKBOOK

COOKSHOP

MICROWAVE COOKBOOK

Cover photograph by Chris Crofton
Inside photography by John Lee

Front cover shows Minestrone Soup (page 17), Hungarian Beef
(page 42) and Grapefruit Cheesecake (page 72)
Title page shows Farmhouse Terrine (page 22) and
Smoked Haddock Pâté (page 31)

Published on behalf of
The Boots Company plc, Nottingham
by Hamlyn Publishing,
a division of The Hamlyn Publishing Group Ltd,
Bridge House, London Road, Twickenham, Middlesex, England

ISBN 0 600 32551 2

First published under the title *Microwave Cookbook*

Set in 10 on 11pt Monophoto Gill Sans
by Servis Filmsetting Ltd, Manchester
Printed in Italy

Contents

Useful Facts & Figures

Notes on metrication

In this book quantities are given in metric and Imperial measures. Exact conversion from Imperial to metric measures does not usually give very convenient working quantities and so the metric measures have been rounded off into units of 25 grams. The table below shows the recommended equivalents.

Ounces	Approx g to nearest whole figure	Recommended conversion to nearest unit of 25
1	28	25
2	57	50
3	85	75
4	113	100
5	142	150
6	170	175
7	198	200
8	227	225
9	255	250
10	283	275
11	312	300
12	340	350
13	368	375
14	396	400
15	425	425
16 (1 lb)	454	450
17	482	475
18	510	500
19	539	550
20 ($1\frac{1}{4}$ lb)	567	575

Note: When converting quantities over 20 oz first add the appropriate figures in the centre column, then adjust to the nearest unit of 25. As a general guide, 1 kg (1000 g) equals 2.2 lb or about 2 lb 3 oz. This method of conversion gives good results in nearly all cases, although in certain pastry and cake recipes a more accurate conversion is necessary to produce a balanced recipe.

Liquid measures

The millilitre has been used in this book and the following table gives a few examples.

Imperial	Approx ml to nearest whole figure	Recommended ml
$\frac{1}{4}$ pint	142	150 ml
$\frac{1}{2}$ pint	283	300 ml
$\frac{3}{4}$ pint	425	450 ml
1 pint	567	600 ml
$1\frac{1}{2}$ pint	851	900 ml
$1\frac{3}{4}$ pints	992	1000 ml (1 litre)

Spoon measures All spoon measures given in this book are level unless otherwise stated.

Can sizes At present, cans are marked with the exact (usually to the nearest whole number) metric equivalent of the Imperial weight of the contents, so we have followed this practice when giving can sizes.

Oven temperatures

The table below gives recommended equivalents.

	°C	°F	Gas
Very cool	110	225	$\frac{1}{4}$
	120	250	$\frac{1}{2}$
Cool	140	275	1
	150	300	2
Moderate	160	325	3
	180	350	4
Moderately hot	190	375	5
	200	400	6
Hot	220	425	7
	230	450	8
Very hot	240	475	9

Note: *When making any of the recipes in this book, only follow one set of measures as they are not interchangeable.*

A selection of utensils to use in the microwave oven.

Introduction

All about microwave ovens

Microwave ovens have opened up a whole new concept in cookery. Originally used mainly in the catering industry, their enormous advantages for home use are now being realised. Not only do they save time, by the speed in which foods cook, but the resulting reduction in fuel costs can be considerable.

For the housewife of today, one of the most valuable aspects of the microwave oven must be its ability to cook foods straight from the freezer; no lengthy defrosting time is required – simply transfer the dish from the freezer to the microwave, and the meal is ready in a matter of minutes.

However, before beginning to use the microwave oven it is important to understand exactly how it operates – and how you should operate it to be assured of maximum success.

The microwave oven

All microwave ovens consist of a basic unit, some with varying levels of power. Some have additional features to the standard model, such as automatic defrosting systems, browning elements, Stay-Hot controls and revolving turntables. In spite of these features the basic principle of microwave cooking remains the same.

How the microwave oven works

(a) A power transformer increases the voltage and supplies the components in the high voltage circuit.
(b) The magnetron converts the electrical energy into electro-magnetic or microwave energy.
(c) The waveguide guides the microwave energy towards the oven cavity.
(d) The wave stirrer (if fitted) distributes the microwaves evenly throughout the oven.
(e) The oven cavity has metallic walls, ceiling and floor which reflect the microwaves.
(f) The oven door is fitted with special seals to ensure that there is the minimum of microwave leakage. At least two cut-out devices are incorporated in the door so that the microwave energy is automatically switched off when the door is opened.

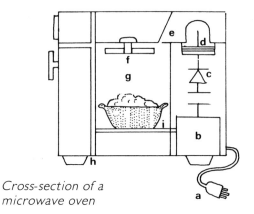

Cross-section of a microwave oven

How the microwave oven cooks or heats food

Microwaves can react in one of three ways when meeting different substances. They are either
(a) reflected or
(b) transmitted or
(c) absorbed.
(d) a combination of these three
(a) Microwaves are reflected by metal or aluminium foil, just as a mirror will reflect light. The oven cavity is made of metal so that the waves are reflected on to the food. It is therefore important to remember not to use metal containers in the oven as the microwaves could be reflected back, causing uneven cooking.
(b) Microwaves are transmitted through substances such as glass, china, ceramics, paper and some plastic, just as light passes

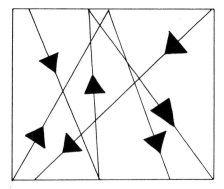

Microwaves being reflected

through a window. Certain glass containers and plastics should only be used for short-time heating, whilst the other types of containers are the most suitable for microwave cooking. Under no circumstances should high lead glasses (e.g. cut glass) be used.

(c) Microwaves are absorbed by food and liquid. The microwaves penetrate about 2.5–3.8 cm/ $1–1\frac{1}{2}$ inches into the food, after which the heat is transferred by conduction.

The microwaves cause the molecules in the food to agitate, producing friction, which creates heat enabling the food to cook quickly.

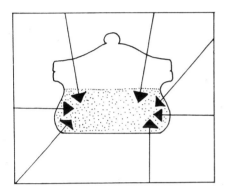

Microwaves being absorbed by food

Safety factors

All microwave ovens are fitted with safety devices ensuring the minimum of microwave leakage. The door is designed so that the microwave energy cuts off immediately it is opened. Some models are designed with drop-down doors; it is important not to stand heavy dishes on these, or even lean on them, as the alignment could be damaged.

Always remember to switch off the oven at the socket outlet, when not in use. With some ovens, if the control switch is accidentally turned on when the microwave is empty, the magnetron could be damaged.

Care and maintenance

Do not attempt to use the oven if it becomes damaged, or try to repair it yourself. Always contact a qualified engineer.

When cleaning the microwave oven, do not allow the cleaning agent to soil or accumulate around the door seal, as this could prevent a tight seal when the door is closed. Never hang damp tea-towels on the oven door.

Never use an abrasive cleaner to clean the interior of the oven, as it can scratch the metallic walls. Do not use aerosols either, as these may penetrate the internal parts of the oven. Simply wipe over with a cloth wrung out in soapy water and rinse with a clean cloth, or follow the manufacturer's instructions. Any persistent smells can be eliminated by heating a cup of lemon juice and water in the microwave.

Cooking utensils

The range of cooking utensils that can be used in the microwave oven is wide. In fact the choice is probably wider than when cooking in a conventional oven. It is, however, important to remember a few basic rules. Always avoid metal dishes, metal baking trays, stainless steel dishes, foil dishes, cast-iron casseroles, dishes trimmed with metallic designs, dishes that have a certain amount of metal actually in the glaze or composition, glassware saucepans with metal screws or handles, metal ties on frozen foods and foil-lined freezer bags. It is sometimes permissible to use small pieces of aluminium foil to protect wing tips of poultry or any parts of food that may cook more quickly, provided the foil does not come into contact with the oven walls. Always read the manufacturer's instruction booklet first, as individual microwave ovens do vary in exactly what is allowed.

China and pottery dishes

Use any ovenproof dishes or containers that you would normally put in a conventional oven, but if using a pottery dish check that it is not porous. Also remember to avoid using dishes trimmed with a metallic design. If you are using the same dish to cook and serve the food, remember that the dish will become hot as it absorbs heat from the food.

Glassware

Ovenproof glassware such as measuring jugs, basins and mixing bowls are ideal for the microwave, provided there are no metal trims or handles with screws.

Paper

Paper plates, cups, paper kitchen towels and napkins are all suitable for use in the microwave, particularly for reheating purposes and short-time cooking. Check plates with a wax coating as they are inclined to melt! Food with a high liquid content, e.g. casseroles, will cause a paper plate to become soggy on reheating. Paper kitchen towels are ideal for cooking fatty foods, e.g. bacon, as they absorb the fat. They are also useful for covering food to prevent any spitting.

Plastics

Only the rigid plastic containers are suitable for the microwave. They should be confined to reheating purposes rather than prolonged cooking. If you are in doubt try a simple test – half-fill a container with water and bring to the boil in the microwave. Check at intervals that the container is still intact.

Plastic wrap

Cling film or freezer film is invaluable for covering dishes. Great care must be taken when removing the film, as trapped steam may spurt out and cause a burn. It is advisable to pierce the film at intervals before cooking.

Plastic bags

Bags such as boil-in-bags, freezer bags and cook-bags may be used provided there are no metal ties. Use elastic bands or string to secure the bags, but make sure they are loosely tied to allow the steam to escape.

Wooden bowls

These are only suitable for short reheating purposes, e.g. when heating bread rolls.

The microwave browning dish

This helps overcome the problem of browning food in the standard microwave oven. Its primary function is to brown meats, fish and poultry, although it can also be used successfully for cooking eggs and frying sandwiches.

The design of the glass-ceramic browning dish incorporates feet, so that the base of the dish does not come into contact with the base of the microwave. The outer side of the base is coated with a special light grey coating which absorbs the microwave energy. When the empty dish is preheated in the microwave, the base becomes hot and changes colour. This dish can be used for casseroles, without the preheating period, provided the entire base is covered with food. The preheating time of the dish varies according to the type of food being cooked and the output of the oven, so always follow the manufacturer's instructions. Do check that your particular model of microwave oven permits the use of

this special dish. Corning Glass International is just one of the companies to manufacture this type of dish.

Microwave/freezer containers

Lakeland Plastics are now producing a range of microwave/freezer containers. These are manufactured from a selection of polythene and polystyrene, with the ability to withstand extreme temperatures, enabling the containers to be used more than once, and to take food in the container straight from the freezer to microwave.

Stirring

The stirring of food is necessary in some recipes e.g. casseroles, soups, sauces, etc. to obtain an even distribution of heat throughout. As the microwaves cook the exposed outer edges of the food first, stirring helps to redistribute the less cooked food.

When stirring, remove the dish from the oven and stir the contents so that the inside food is moved to the outer edges of the dish and vice versa.

Rearrangement and turning of food

When it is not possible to stir the food, the food must be rearranged in the microwave, for the same reason. This applies to dishes such as crème caramel, crème brûlée, etc.

If using individual dishes, it is necessary to rearrange the positions during cooking, so they can all cook evenly. A large dish, e.g. a cheesecake, will simply require turning during cooking. This may not be necessary with turntables.

Standing time

To varying degrees all food continues to cook once removed from the oven and it is sometimes necessary to have a standing period, to allow the cooking to finish e.g. a joint of meat. (See chart on page 40.) Sometimes the standing time comes during the cooking time, e.g. a cheesecake requires a standing period since the mixture cannot be stirred and the dish can only be rotated. The standing time allows the heat to transfer naturally into the cooler centre of the food.

With smaller items such as vegetables the time between being removed from the microwave and being served is sufficient for heat transference. The denser the food the longer the standing time.

Defrosting frozen food in the microwave

The freezer and the microwave oven are natural partners. Frozen food can be taken from the freezer and put straight into the microwave oven, provided it is not in a foil container or a freezer bag lined with foil and all the metal fastenings have been removed.

Defrosting in the standard microwave oven needs more attention than in a microwave with an automatic defrosting system, because the defrosting times and the standing times have to be alternated manually. The standing time allows the heat to be conducted into the centre of the frozen food, without actual cooking taking place. If food was defrosted without standing times, it would be unevenly thawed.

For defrosting times of meat see page 40 and chicken see page 32. Many convenience foods give suggested times on the packet.

If you have to transfer a block of frozen food to a different container for defrosting, choose a container to fit the shape of the frozen food. If the dish has too wide a surface area, the outside of the food will defrost, covering the base of the dish, and this will cook while the centre of the food remains frozen.

Factors influencing microwave cooking

Starting temperatures
The colder the food when put into the microwave oven, the longer cooking time is required; so allowances must be made if using food straight from the refrigerator or freezer.

Density
The denser the food, the longer it will take to cook.

Shapes
Always aim for uniform shapes, especially with joints of meat. If one end of the joint is much thinner, this will obviously cook more quickly than the denser part of the joint. However, there are some joints which are never uniform, e.g. a leg of lamb. To overcome this problem, it is a good idea to bone and stuff the joint or bone and tie it into a neat shape. If your microwave oven permits the use of foil, then protect the thinner part of the leg with foil to slow down the cooking time on the covered part.

Poultry should always have the legs and wings well tucked into the body. If these protrude then they will cook well in advance of the rest of the bird.

Frozen casseroles are normally an ideal shape to allow even defrosting.

Timing
This is probably the most crucial part of microwave cookery and it will often take a while to adjust to it. The manufacturer's recommendations should always be used for guidance. The levels of microwave energy vary with the different makes of oven and each manufacturer provides a guide to timings for their particular models. Always read the instructions carefully.

Remember it is better to undercook than to overcook. Undercooked food can always be rectified but, once overcooked, the food becomes dehydrated and cannot be saved.

Unlike conventional cooking, the microwave cooking time increases with any additional items in the oven; for example, two mugs of coffee will take longer than one mug.

Cooking time is also affected by the shape and size of the cooking utensil used. If you are going to use different utensils from those stipulated in the recipes, check the timing carefully.

Power settings
All the recipes in this book were tested on full power in an oven with an output of 600 watts. Check the output of your oven and adjust the cooking times slightly if it has a different output. If the output is higher the cooking times will be shorter; if the output is lower the times will be longer. All the recipes in this book were cooked most successfully and with maximum speed using full power. Lower power settings are useful for defrosting foods or for lengthening the cooking time if you want to leave the dish to cook unattended for some time.

Soups & Starters

Home-made soups are delicious cooked in the microwave. They can be prepared in advance, then reheated in the microwave. Always remember that food cooked or reheated in the microwave becomes extremely hot, so allow it to cool slightly before serving. Pâté is always popular and, like many other starters, it is easy to prepare in the microwave. So there is no excuse to cut out the first course of the meal!

SPINACH SOUP

SERVES 4

(Illustrated overleaf)

25 g/ l oz butter
25 g/ l oz flour
450 ml/¾ pint milk
300 ml/½ pint hot chicken stock
½ teaspoon nutmeg
l tablespoon grated onion
salt and freshly ground black pepper
l (227-g/8-oz) packet frozen chopped
spinach, thawed
double cream to swirl

Place the butter in a mixing bowl and melt in the microwave for l minute. Stir in the flour until well mixed, then gradually add the milk, stock, nutmeg, onion and seasoning, whisking well. Cook in the microwave for 7 minutes, whisking 3 times to prevent lumps forming. Add the spinach and mix well. Cook for a further 4 minutes in the microwave. Allow to cool slightly before liquidising. Reheat in the microwave if necessary. Swirl cream into the soup just before serving.

MINESTRONE SOUP

SERVES 4

l tablespoon oil
l red or green pepper, seeded and
cut into strips
l carrot, sliced
l stick celery, sliced
l onion, sliced
l potato, peeled and chopped
l clove garlic, crushed
900 ml/ l½ pints hot ham stock
25 g/ l oz spaghetti, broken
into pieces or pasta shapes
l (226-g/8-oz) can tomatoes
l leek, shredded
Garnish:
grated Parmesan cheese
chopped parsley

Place the oil, prepared vegetables and garlic in a mixing bowl and cook in the microwave for 3 minutes. Stir well, add the stock and spaghetti, then cook in the microwave for 13 minutes, stirring twice during cooking. Add the tomatoes and leek and cook for a further 7 minutes in the microwave, stirring once. Allow to stand for a few minutes before serving. Garnish with Parmesan and chopped parsley.

Note: You can add all sorts of vegetables and a wide variety of pasta shapes to minestrone soup. Shredded cabbage, peas, French beans or canned haricot beans are all suitable ingredients.

Minestrone Soup

SWEETCORN SOUP
SERVES 4

15 g/½ oz butter
1 medium onion, finely chopped
50 g/2 oz bacon, chopped
15 g/½ oz cornflour
300 ml/½ pint milk
2 (170-g/6-oz) packets frozen
sweetcorn, thawed
300 ml/½ pint hot chicken stock
salt and freshly ground black pepper

Place the butter, onion and bacon in a mixing bowl and cook in the microwave for 1 minute. Blend the cornflour and milk together and pour on to the bacon and onion. Cook in the microwave for 4 minutes, stirring twice during cooking. Whisk the sauce and add the sweetcorn, reserving a little for garnish, and stock. Return to the microwave for 3 minutes. Allow to cool slightly then liquidise the soup. Adjust the seasoning and reheat in the microwave if necessary. Garnish with reserved sweetcorn.

Variations
Tuna and sweetcorn soup: The combination of canned tuna fish and sweetcorn goes to make a tasty soup which is ideal for lunch or supper. Drain and flake 1 (198-g/7-oz) can tuna fish and add it to the liquidised soup. Reheat before serving, with warm crusty bread.

Chicken and sweetcorn soup: Omit the bacon from the above recipe. Add 450 g/1 lb chopped cooked chicken meat (without skin and bones) to the liquidised soup and reheat before serving. Sprinkle with a little chopped parsley to add colour.

Clockwise from top right: Cauliflower Soup (overleaf), Sweetcorn Soup and Spinach Soup (previous page).

CAULIFLOWER SOUP
SERVES 4
(Illustrated on previous page) Veg Version

50 g/2 oz butter Olive Oil?
1 onion, finely diced
2 tablespoons flour
750 ml/1¼ pints hot chicken stock Veg stock?
1 (339-g/12-oz) packet frozen
cauliflower florets
salt and freshly ground black pepper
Garnish:
2 tablespoons single cream X Grated Cheese
chopped parsley Chives?

Place the butter and onion in a mixing bowl and cook in the microwave for 2 minutes. Stir in the flour, then pour in the stock and return to the microwave for 3 minutes. Place the frozen cauliflower in a cook-bag, secure loosely with an elastic band and cook in the microwave for 9 minutes, turning 3 times. Add the cauliflower florets to the sauce and cook in the microwave for 2 minutes. Allow to cool slightly then liquidise or sieve the soup. Adjust the seasoning and reheat in the microwave if necessary. Just before serving, stir in the cream and chopped parsley.

Note: If you like, stir 50 g/2 oz grated cheese into the soup before adding the cream. Alternatively, top each individual portion with crumbled Stilton cheese.

FRENCH ONION SOUP
SERVES 4

50 g/2 oz butter
350 g/12 oz onions, thinly sliced
2 tablespoons flour
generous litre/2 pints hot beef stock
salt and freshly ground black pepper
3 tablespoons sherry
Topping:
4 thick slices French bread
100 g/4 oz Cheddar cheese, sliced

On a conventional cooker, melt the butter in a medium-sized saucepan. Add the onions and cook until brown, then stir in the flour to absorb most of the butter.

Gradually stir in the beef stock and seasoning. Transfer the soup to a mixing bowl. Cook in the microwave for 5 minutes. Stir in the sherry and allow to stand for a few minutes before serving.

For the topping, toast one side of the bread slices, top the untoasted sides with cheese and cook under a hot grill until golden. Float the cheese on bread in individual bowls of soup just before it is served.

Note: It is necessary to fry the onions initially in order to obtain a good rich brown colour for the soup.

French Onion Soup

FARMHOUSE TERRINE

SERVES 4

100 g/4 oz ox kidney, chopped
225 g/8 oz lamb's liver, chopped
225 g/8 oz boneless pork, chopped
1 small onion, finely chopped
5 rashers streaky bacon, derinded
2–3 bay leaves
50 g/2 oz fresh breadcrumbs
salt and freshly ground black pepper
pinch basil
1 clove garlic, crushed
1 egg, beaten

Place the chopped offal, meat and onion in an ovenproof pie dish and cook in the microwave for 5 minutes, stirring once during cooking. Stretch the bacon rasher using the back of a knife. Place the bay leaves on the base of an ovenproof soufflé dish or microwave-proof terrine. Line the dish with the bacon rashers.

Mix the meats with the remaining ingredients and place in the lined dish, smoothing the surface with a knife. Cover with cling film or greaseproof paper and cook in the microwave for 10 minutes. Allow to stand for 5 minutes. Cover with a clean piece of greaseproof paper and place a heavy weight on a saucer or small plate on top. Allow to cool then refrigerate overnight. Turn out carefully. Serve with French bread and a salad.

Variations
Mixed herb terrine: Add 4 tablespoons chopped mixed fresh herbs to the mixture. Include parsley, thyme, tarragon, sage, marjoram, rosemary, basil or chives.
Peppered terrine: Add 2 tablespoons lightly crushed green peppercorns to the mixture, continue as above.

CHICKEN LIVER PÂTÉ

SERVES 4

25 g/ 1 oz butter
1 tablespoon oil
1 clove garlic, crushed
1 medium onion, finely chopped
350 g/ 12 oz chicken livers, washed
and dried
salt and freshly ground black pepper
freshly ground nutmeg
1 tablespoon brandy
100 g/ 4 oz butter
Garnish:
lemon
cress

Place the butter, oil, garlic and onion in a round ovenproof dish and cook in the microwave for 3 minutes, stirring once during cooking. Add the chicken livers and seasonings, continue to cook in the microwave for 4 minutes, stirring twice. Stir in the brandy, cool slightly and liquidise until smooth. Place in 4 ramekin dishes and smooth the tops.

Put the butter in a glass jug and melt in the microwave for 1 minute or until melted. Pour over the individual pâtés and place a lemon slice in the butter. Chill until set and garnish with cress.

Variations

Tarragon chicken liver pâté: Add 2 tablespoons chopped fresh tarragon to the puréed mixture before putting it into the ramekins.

Citrus chicken liver pâté: Add the grated rind of 1 small lemon to the purée mixture before putting it into the ramekins.

EGG MOUSSE

SERVES 4

25 g/ 1 oz butter
1 clove garlic, crushed
3 tablespoons flour
300 ml/$\frac{1}{2}$ pint milk
4 hard-boiled eggs, chopped
2 eggs, separated
15 g/$\frac{1}{2}$ oz gelatine
2 tablespoons hot water
Garnish:
quartered hard-boiled eggs
watercress sprigs

Melt the butter in a mixing bowl in the microwave for 1 minute. Add the garlic and stir in the flour. Gradually add the milk, whisking well, and return to the microwave for 4 minutes. Whisk the sauce 4 times during cooking and again very well at the end of the cooking time.

Add the chopped hard-boiled eggs and egg yolks to the sauce and cool slightly. Dissolve the gelatine in the hot water, add to the sauce and leave in a cool place until half set. Whisk the egg whites until they form stiff peaks then fold into the half set mixture. Pour into a lightly oiled 1.5-litre/2$\frac{1}{2}$-pint mould and leave to set in a cool place.

Turn out on to a suitable serving dish and garnish with quartered hard-boiled eggs and sprigs of watercress. Serve with Melba toast.

Variations

Danish egg mousse: Beat 100 g/4 oz crumbled Danish blue cheese into the hot sauce before adding the eggs. Stir in 2 tablespoons chopped chives, then continue as in the main recipe.

ARTICHOKES VINAIGRETTE

SERVES 4

4 globe artichokes
6 tablespoons lemon juice
8 tablespoons water
8 tablespoons olive oil
I clove garlic, crushed
salt and freshly ground black pepper
I teaspoon caster sugar

Trim any long thick stalks off the artichokes, then wash them thoroughly and shake the excess water out of the leaves. Snip the tips off the leaves (use a pair of kitchen scissors), then place the artichokes in a cook-bag and sprinkle in 2 tablespoons of the lemon juice and the water. Secure the opening loosely with an elastic band, then cook on full power for 20 to 25 minutes. To make sure the artichokes are cooked, try pulling off one of the leaves; it should come away fairly easily.

While the artichokes are cooking put all the remaining ingredients in a screw-topped jar and shake thoroughly until the dressing is combined.

Trim the artichokes: remove the very large outer leaves around the base to give a neat shape. Carefully separate the leaves and pull out the cluster which covers the choke in the middle of the vegetable. By pulling this out the hairy, inedible choke (seen in the halved vegetable in the picture) should be removed but carefully take out any remaining bits without damaging the prime part – the artichoke bottom.

Place the artichokes on individual serving plates and spoon the vinaigrette dressing into the middle. Serve at once.

GRAPEFRUIT WITH VERMOUTH

SERVES 4

2 tablespoons white vermouth
2 tablespoons clear honey
2 grapefruit
Garnish:
mint leaf

Mix together the vermouth and honey. Halve the grapefruit and loosen the segments then carefully spoon the vermouth mixture over them.

Heat two halves at a time in the microwave on a double thickness of kitchen paper, allowing I minute for each pair. Half turn the grapefruit after 30 seconds. Serve hot garnished with a mint leaf.

BAKED AVOCADO WITH SHRIMPS

SERVES 4

150 ml/$\frac{1}{4}$ pint milk
7 g/$\frac{1}{4}$ oz butter
I tablespoon flour
$\frac{1}{2}$ (212-g/7$\frac{1}{2}$-oz) can shrimps, drained
pinch cayenne pepper
salt and freshly ground black pepper
few drops lemon juice
2 teaspoons tomato purée
2 ripe avocado pears
Topping:
I–2 tablespoons fresh breadcrumbs

Place the milk in a measuring jug and heat in the microwave for 30 seconds. Mix the butter with the flour then whisk gradually into the milk. Return to the microwave for I minute or until thickened. Add the shrimps, cayenne pepper, seasoning, lemon juice and tomato purée.

Cut the avocados in half and remove the stones. Brush the cut surfaces with a little lemon juice to prevent discoloration. Pile the shrimp filling in the centre of each avocado and sprinkle with breadcrumbs. Place the pear halves in a circle on a sheet of kitchen paper and return to the microwave for 2 minutes, stopping after I minute to alter the position of the avocado halves. Serve at once.

Artichokes Vinaigrette

Fish Dishes

Fish cooked in the microwave retains all its natural flavour and nutrients. Cook-bags have proved very successful for cooking fish, especially whole fish such as trout.
If you are cooking a large piece of fish, try and arrange it into a uniform shape by tucking in any thin parts such as the tail. This will prevent the thinner parts from overcooking.
Be careful not to overcook fish as it will toughen and dry out. Always undercook slightly, as the fish will continue to cook in its own heat once removed from the oven.

KEDGEREE

SERVES 4

450 g| 1 lb smoked haddock fillets
1 tablespoon lemon juice
600 ml| 1 pint boiling water
2 tablespoons chopped parsley
25 g| 1 oz butter
1 onion, finely chopped
175 g|6 oz long-grain rice
bay leaf
3 hard-boiled eggs, chopped
salt and freshly ground black pepper
Garnish:
chopped parsley
lemon slices

Place the fish in an oblong dish together with the lemon juice, boiling water and parsley. Cook in the microwave for 4 minutes, turning the dish once. Remove the fish and reserve the stock. Skin and flake the fish, removing any bones.

Heat the butter in a casserole dish in the microwave for 1 minute then add the onion and cook in the microwave for 2 minutes. Add the rice and bay leaf; pour over the fish stock and cook in the microwave for a further 15 minutes or until the liquid is absorbed.

Remove the bay leaf then mix in the fish and hard-boiled eggs. Season with salt and freshly ground black pepper. Garnish with parsley and lemon slices.

COQUILLES SAINT JACQUES

SERVES 2

25 g| 1 oz butter
1 small onion, finely chopped
100 g|4 oz button mushrooms, sliced
150 ml|$\frac{1}{4}$ pint dry white wine
4 scallops, washed and quartered
1 teaspoon lemon juice
2 tablespoons chopped parsley
salt and freshly ground black pepper
bay leaf · 15 g|$\frac{1}{2}$ oz flour
3 tablespoons single cream
2 tablespoons dry breadcrumbs

Place half the butter and the onion in an ovenproof dish and cook in the microwave for 3 minutes. Stir in the mushrooms, wine, scallops, lemon juice, parsley, seasoning and bay leaf. Cook for 4 minutes, stirring once. Remove and discard the bay leaf.

Place the remaining butter in a measuring jug and melt in the microwave for 30 seconds. Stir in the flour and mix to a smooth paste. Strain the liquor from the scallops into the jug, stir in the cream and pour over the scallops. Transfer to two scallop shells or individual dishes and sprinkle with the breadcrumbs. Return to the microwave for 1–2 minutes, then serve.

Kedgeree

PAUPIETTES OF PLAICE IN WINE SAUCE

SERVES 4

8 plaice fillets, skinned
150 ml/¼ pint white wine
150 ml/¼ chicken stock
bay leaf
blade mace
few peppercorns
salt and freshly ground black pepper
slice lemon
few drops lemon juice
15 g/½ oz butter
15 g/½ oz flour
Garnish:
few white grapes
watercress
croûtons

Roll the plaice fillets and secure with a wooden cocktail stick if necessary. Place the fish in a shallow dish and pour over the wine, stock, bay leaf, mace, peppercorns, salt and pepper, lemon slice and juice. Cover with greaseproof paper and cook in the microwave for 5 minutes, turning the dish once during cooking. Carefully drain off the liquor and reserve. Keep the fish hot.

Mix the butter and flour together in the basin and pour the strained liquor over, whisking well. Cook in the microwave for 1 minute, stir and cook for a further minute. Pour over the plaice and garnish with grapes, watercress and croûtons.

SAVOURY FISH CRUMBLE

SERVES 4

50 g/2 oz butter
1 medium onion, chopped
1 tablespoon chopped green pepper
450 g/1 lb cod fillet, skinned and boned
salt and freshly ground black pepper
75 g/3 oz fresh brown breadcrumbs
grated rind of 1 lemon
50 g/2 oz red Leicester cheese, grated
2 tablespoons chopped parsley

Place the butter in a casserole dish and melt in the microwave for 1 minute. Add the onion and green pepper and cook in the microwave for 4 minutes, stirring twice. Add the flaked fish and season lightly. Cook in the microwave for a further 4 minutes, stirring every minute.

Mix together the remaining ingredients and cover the fish with the mixture. Heat in the microwave for 4 minutes, turning the dish twice.

Note: For an economical mid-week meal, use boneless frozen coley steaks instead of the cod in the above recipe. Cut the fish into chunks when it is half frozen. Allow an extra 2–3 minutes cooking time so that the coley defrosts before cooking.

DEVILLED CRAB

SERVES 2

15 g/½ oz butter
1 small shallot, finely chopped
150 g/5 oz crabmeat
1 tablespoon dry sherry
2 tablespoons fresh breadcrumbs
pinch cayenne pepper
few drops Worcestershire sauce
1 teaspoon Dijon mustard
salt and freshly ground black pepper
Topping:
1 tablespoon fresh breadcrumbs
1 tablespoon grated Parmesan cheese
1 tablespoon chopped parsley
Garnish:
lemon slices
watercress sprigs

Place the butter and shallot in a basin and cook in the microwave for 3 minutes. Stir in the remaining ingredients until well combined.

Divide the mixture between 2 scallop shells or shell-shaped dishes. Mix the topping ingredients and sprinkle over the devilled crab. Return to the microwave and heat for 1–2 minutes, until hot. Garnish with quartered lemon slices and watercress sprigs. Serve with hot crusty bread, hot buttered toast or warm Granary rolls.

Note: Frozen crabmeat can be used instead of canned fish in the above recipe. Alternatively, substitute canned tuna fish (drained of oil or brine) or prawns for the crabmeat.

TROUT IN WHITE WINE

SERVES 4

salt and freshly ground black pepper
4 trout, cleaned and boned
25 g/ I oz butter, melted
I tablespoon chopped parsley
grated rind of I lemon
150 ml/¼ pint dry white wine
I teaspoon cornflour

Season the inside of the trout and brush with melted butter. Sprinkle the parsley and lemon rind inside the trout.

Place 2 fish in the cook-bag with the wine and secure loosely with an elastic band. Cook in the microwave for 3 minutes. Carefully split the bag and remove the fish to a serving dish.

Transfer the liquid to another cook-bag and cook the remaining trout in this in the microwave for 3 minutes. Reserve the cooking liquid and place in a pudding basin. Blend the cornflour with a little of the liquid then stir into the rest of the liquid and thicken in the microwave for 30 seconds. Pour over the trout before serving.

Smoked Haddock Pâté

SMOKED HADDOCK PÂTÉ

SERVES 4

450 g/ I lb smoked haddock fillets,
skinned
2 tablespoons finely chopped onion
225 g/ 8 oz cream cheese
salt and freshly ground black pepper
50 g/ 2 oz butter
Garnish:
lemon slices
parsley sprigs

Cut the fish into chunks and place in a casserole dish together with the onion. Cook in the microwave for 5 minutes, stirring twice.

Cool and liquidise the fish with the cream cheese. Taste and season before pressing into individual ramekin dishes or a large serving dish.

Melt the butter in a measuring jug for 30 seconds, or until melted. Pour the butter over the pâté. Garnish with lemon slices and chill until firm. Add sprigs of parsley before serving. Offer crusty rolls, butter and salad ingredients with the pâté.

SOUSED MACKEREL

SERVES 4

100 g/ 4 oz onion, sliced
150 ml/¼ pint vinegar
150 ml/¼ pint water
2 bay leaves
¼ teaspoon salt
freshly ground black pepper
4 mackerel, cleaned and boned
Garnish:
lemon wedges
watercress

Place the onion in a casserole dish and pour over the vinegar and water. Add the bay leaves, salt and freshly ground black pepper.

Place 2 mackerel in the liquid and cook in the microwave for 8 minutes, turning the fish four times during cooking. Remove the fish from the cooking liquid and cook the second pair for approximately 8 minutes. (The second pair of fish may not take quite as long as the first pair since the liquid will have already been heated.) Serve cold, garnished with lemon and watercress.

Poultry & Game

Poultry is a tender meat, therefore it cooks very well in the microwave oven. Bones and joints which protrude are prone to overcooking but boneless pieces of chicken, boned whole chickens and small game birds cook quite successfully. If the poultry is cooked in a sauce the fact that it does not brown does not matter. Alternatively, the bird can always be browned under a grill or in a very hot oven.

ROASTING CHICKEN AND DUCK

Cut of meat	Weight of joint	Total microwave cooking time	Total resting time	Microwave cooking time per 0.5 kg/1 lb	Additional time from frozen		
					Total microwave defrosting time	Resting time	Microwave defrosting time per 0.5 kg/1 lb
Chicken, whole, unboned	1.5 kg/3¼ lb	15 minutes	30 minutes	4½–5 minutes	12 minutes	40 minutes	3½–4 minutes
Duck, whole, unboned	2 kg/3¾ lb	20 minutes	20 minutes	4–5 minutes	16 minutes	45 minutes	3½–4 minutes

CHICKEN WITH VEGETABLES IN WINE

SERVES 4

1 (1.5-kg/3¼-lb) chicken
25 g/1 oz butter
225 g/8 oz small onions, peeled
225 g/8 oz carrots, thickly sliced
100 g/4 oz streaky bacon, chopped
1 green pepper, deseeded and chopped
2 sticks celery, sliced
100 g/4 oz small button mushrooms
bay leaf
salt and freshly ground black pepper
2 tablespoons flour
300 ml/½ pint medium dry white wine
300 ml/½ pint chicken stock

Tie the legs of the chicken together firmly to hold them as close to the body of the bird as possible. Place the chicken on an upturned pie dish in a larger oblong dish. Cook in the microwave for 5 minutes, turning the dish round and the bird over at the end of the cooking time. Continue to cook in the microwave for a further 10 minutes, again turning the bird over 4 times and turning the dish round twice during the cooking time.

Wrap the chicken in a double thickness of foil with the shiny side inwards and allow to stand for 20–30 minutes before serving.

Melt the butter in the shallow dish in the microwave for 1 minute then add the onions, carrots, bacon, pepper and celery. Cook in the microwave for a further 5 minutes before adding the mushrooms and bay leaf. Season lightly and stir in the flour. Add the wine and stock and thicken in the microwave for 10 minutes, stirring twice.

Brown the chicken under a conventional grill, if liked, and then place in a serving dish. Arrange the vegetables round the chicken and spoon over the sauce.

ROLLED GALANTINE OF CHICKEN

SERVES 4

*1 frozen (1.5-kg/3½-lb) chicken,
defrosted (see method) and boned
100 g/4 oz onion, finely chopped
100 g/4 oz cooked ham, chopped
100 g/4 oz cooked tongue, chopped
225 g/8 oz sausagemeat
1 tablespoon chopped fresh
mixed herbs
2 tablespoons sherry
2 tablespoons chopped black olives
1 tablespoon chopped stuffed olives
salt and freshly ground black pepper*
Garnish:
*tomato wedges
watercress sprigs*

To defrost the chicken, place the bird, breast-side uppermost, in an oblong dish, having first opened the bag and removed any metal ties from the bird.

Defrost in the microwave for 2 minutes and turn the chicken over, breast side down. Return to the microwave for 2 minutes more. Turn the bird over and rest for 5 minutes. Repeat this process 4 times more. Wrap the chicken in a double thickness of foil, placing the shiny side inwards to reflect the heat back into the bird. Leave to stand for 20 minutes then unwrap and remove the giblets. Rinse the cavity with boiling water.

Place the onion in a soufflé dish and cook in the microwave for 5 minutes. Add the ham, tongue and sausagemeat. Mix well then stir in the herbs, sherry and chopped olives; season lightly.

Bone the chicken and place, skin side down, on a board. Spread the stuffing out over the chicken, splitting the legs down one side. Roll the chicken up from head to tail, tucking in any protruding flesh, to form a long thin sausage. Sew up firmly with a large needle threaded with double cotton and place on a large oval meat dish. Cook in the microwave for 15 minutes, turning the dish round 3 times and turning the chicken over every 5 minutes. Remove any excess drippings during the cooking time. Remove the string and wrap the chicken in foil, shiny side inwards, then allow to stand for 15 minutes; garnish and serve.

CHICKEN TANDOORI
SERVES 4

4 chicken joints
150 ml/¼ pint plain yogurt
grated rind of ½ lemon
1 tablespoon ground ginger
½ teaspoon turmeric
½ teaspoon garlic salt
salt and freshly ground black pepper

Make slashes into the chicken at intervals, taking care only to penetrate halfway through the flesh. Mix the remaining ingredients together and spread over the chicken, pressing well in between the cuts. Cover with cling film and leave overnight.

Place the chicken in a shallow dish, cover with the yogurt mixture and cook for 5 minutes, give the dish a quarter turn and continue to cook for a further 5 minutes. Alter the position of the chicken pieces and return to the microwave for 10 minutes, giving the dish a quarter turn after 5 minutes.

Serve hot, with plain cooked rice and a side salad or the spicy raita recipe below, if you like.

Spicy raita: Trim and chop 1 bunch spring onions. Peel and chop 1 small cucumber then mix it with the onions, 1 teaspoon chopped fresh mint, ¼ teaspoon chilli powder and 1 crushed clove garlic. Add 150 ml/¼ pint thoroughly chilled natural yogurt, mix well and serve sprinkled with a little extra chilli powder.

CHICKEN AND WATER CHESTNUT PILAF
SERVES 4

1 onion, finely chopped
15 g/½ oz butter
1 tablespoon oil
4 chicken breasts
300 ml/½ pint apple juice
¼ teaspoon turmeric
salt and freshly ground black pepper
1 (227-g/8-oz) can water chestnuts,
drained and sliced
10 stuffed olives, halved
1 tablespoon cornflour
Pilaf rice:
300 ml/½ pint hand-hot water
100 g/4 oz long-grain rice
¼ teaspoon turmeric
Garnish:
chopped parsley

Place the onion, butter and oil in a casserole and cook in the microwave for 5 minutes, stirring twice. Add the chicken to the dish and cook for 4 minutes, turning the chicken over after 2 minutes.

Stir in the apple juice, turmeric and seasoning and cook for a further 2 minutes. Blend the cornflour with a little water and stir into the chicken mixture. Cover and allow to stand while the rice is cooking.

For the pilaf rice, place all the ingredients in a heatproof measuring jug and cook for 10 minutes. Stir well and serve with the chicken mixture piled on top. Garnish with chopped parsley.

DUCK À L'ORANGE

1 (2–2.5 kg/4–4½ lb) duck
2 large oranges
bay leaf
salt and freshly ground black pepper
300 ml/½ pint boiling water
2 tablespoons flour
1 chicken stock cube
Garnish:
orange slices, peeled
chopped parsley
watercress sprigs

Remove the giblets from the duck and set them aside to make the sauce. Prick the skin of the bird all over. Prick one of the oranges all over, then place it inside the duck with the bay leaf. Place the duck, breast side down, in a shallow ovenproof glass dish and cover it with cling film, allowing a small gap for the steam to escape. Cook for 5 minutes then turn the duck over so that the breast meat is up and continue to cook for a further 20 minutes, turning the dish round once during cooking.

Remove the duck from the dish and place it, breast side uppermost, on a roasting rack in a roasting tin. Rub salt into the skin and cook in a very hot oven (240 C, 475 F, gas 9) for 15–20 minutes. At the end of the cooking time the duck should be golden brown and crisp.

While the duck is cooking, place the reserved giblets with the pared rind from the remaining orange in a basin. Pour in the boiling water and cook in the microwave for 15 minutes. Remove and strain the stock.

Place a couple of spoonfuls of the duck juices in a basin or large jug and stir in the flour, then pour in the hot stock, stirring continuously to prevent lumps from forming. Crumble in the stock cube. Squeeze the juice from the orange and pour it into the sauce, then cook for 5 minutes.

Transfer the duck to a heated serving platter, or cut it into four joints and arrange these on a serving dish. Add a garnish of orange slices, rolled in chopped parsley, and watercress then serve accompanied by the prepared sauce.

PIGEONS IN RED WINE

SERVES 4

25 g/ 1 oz butter
1 tablespoon oil
2 pigeons, drawn and trussed
4 rashers streaky bacon
1 onion, finely chopped
1 tablespoon flour
2 tablespoons redcurrant jelly
150 ml/¼ pint red wine
150 ml/¼ pint stock
1 tablespoon tomato purée
salt and finely ground black pepper
100 g/ 4 oz button mushrooms
50 g/ 2 oz stuffed olives
2 tablespoons chopped parsley
Garnish:
watercress

Place an empty browning dish, without the lid, in the microwave and heat for 4 minutes. Add the butter and oil then place the pigeons, each wrapped in 2 rashers of bacon, in the heated dish. Cook in the microwave for 4 minutes, turning the birds frequently, so they are browned on all sides. Remove the birds and stir in the onion. Cover and cook in the microwave for 2 minutes. Stir in the flour, redcurrant jelly, wine, stock, tomato purée and seasoning and return to the microwave for 2 minutes. Stir well and return the birds to the dish. Cover and cook in the microwave for 8 minutes, turning the dish and the birds after 4 minutes. Cook for a further 4 minutes then add the mushrooms, olives and parsley. Cook for 4 minutes. Allow to stand for a few minutes before serving. Garnish with watercress.

Note: If the birds are too high in the dish for the lid to be used, cover with cling film. Timing of this dish may vary according to the age of the pigeons.

Above: Pigeons in Red Wine in preparation;
Opposite: the finished dish

Meat Dishes

The microwave really comes into its own in this chapter. Joints of meat are literally cooked in minutes: for example a 1.25-kg/ 2¾-lb piece of topside can be cooked in a total of 15 minutes! A chart giving the cooking times and defrosting times for various meats can be found overleaf. Frozen meat can be successfully defrosted in the microwave in minutes, saving the endless hours normally spent on defrosting meat.
When cooking casseroles use good quality meat as the rapid cooking of the microwave is not suitable for the tougher cuts. Remember also that small pieces of meat cook more quickly than large pieces. If you want to brown chops or joints, then you can use a microwave oven browning dish or simply flash the meat under a very hot grill.

BEEF OLIVES
SERVES 4

25 g/ 1 oz dry white breadcrumbs
50 g/ 2 oz mushrooms, finely chopped
½ teaspoon dried mixed herbs
1 tablespoon lemon juice
3 tablespoons milk
salt and freshly ground black pepper
450 g/ 1 lb topside, thinly sliced
25 g/ 1 oz butter
225 g/ 8 oz small onions
2 tablespoons flour
450 ml/¾ pint good brown stock
2 tablespoons dry sherry
100 g/ 4 oz small button mushrooms
Garnish:
chopped parsley

Mix the first five ingredients together, season to taste and divide between the slices of topside. Roll the meat up, folding the sides in to form neat parcels and secure with string.

Place the butter in a casserole dish and melt in the microwave for 1 minute, then add the onions and cook for a further 5 minutes. Stir in the flour and carefully add the stock, sherry and mushrooms. Stir well.

Place the meat in the dish with the sauce and cook in the microwave for 15 minutes, turning the meat over and round every 2 minutes. Leave to stand for 3 minutes before transferring to a serving dish. Garnish with a little chopped parsley and serve at once.

PEPPERED STEAKS WITH MADEIRA

SERVES 4

50 g/2 oz butter
1 clove garlic, crushed
2 large onions, sliced
1 green pepper, sliced
1 red pepper, sliced
5 tablespoons Madeira
salt
2 tablespoons Marmite
4 (175-g/6-oz) rump steaks
20 black peppercorns, crushed
Garnish:
watercress

Melt the butter in an oblong dish in a microwave for 2 minutes. Add the garlic, onions, green and red pepper. Toss well then place the dish in a cook-bag (or cover the dish with the bag split) and cook in the microwave for 5 minutes. Stir in the vegetables and add 4 tablespoons of the Madeira. Season lightly with salt and replace the dish in the cook-bag. Continue to cook in the microwave for 5 minutes.

Mix the Marmite with the remaining Madeira and brush each side of the steaks with this mixture. Place them on the bed of vegetables and sprinkle the crushed peppercorns over the top. Return to the microwave and cook for 4 minutes, turning and rearranging the steaks once during cooking. (If the steaks are not cooked enough after 4 minutes for your liking, cook for a little longer.) Garnish with watercress.

MEAT ROASTING CHART

Cut of meat	Weight of joint	Total microwave cooking time	Total resting time	Microwave cooking time per 0.5 kg/1 lb	Additional time from frozen		
					Total microwave defrosting time	Resting time	Microwave defrosting time per 0.5 kg/1 lb
Beef, topside (medium rare)	1.25 kg/2¾ lb	15 minutes	35–40 minutes	5 minutes	16 minutes	60 minutes	5 minutes
Beef, rolled rib roast (medium)	1.5 kg/3 lb	20 minutes	30–40 minutes	6–7 minutes	16 minutes	55 minutes	5 minutes
Lamb, unboned fillet off leg (well cooked)	1 kg/2 lb	15 minutes	35 minutes	7 minutes	9 minutes	35 minutes	4–5 minutes
Lamb, shoulder boned and rolled (well cooked)	1.25 kg/2½ lb	20 minutes	30–40 minutes	8 minutes	10 minutes	45–55 minutes	4 minutes
Pork, unboned fillet off leg	1.5 kg/3 lb	25 minutes	30–40 minutes	8–9 minutes	12 minutes	40–50 minutes	4–5 minutes

Instructions for roasting a joint

1. Calculate the cooking time required (see chart).
2. Place the joint on an upturned plate in a large dish. Cook in the microwave for approximately 5 minutes at a time, allowing a 5-minute resting time between each cooking period, until the total microwave cooking time is reached.
3. Wrap in foil (with the shiny side inwards) and stand for 15–30 minutes, or the remaining resting time, until the meat is cooked through.

This is only a guide, as times will vary according to personal taste and the shape and size of the meat.

Instructions for defrosting and cooking a frozen joint

1. Weigh the joint to determine the time necessary to defrost it prior to cooking (see chart).
2. Place the joint on an upturned plate in a large dish and defrost in the microwave for approximately 5 minutes at a time, allowing resting periods of 5 minutes between each, until the total calculated defrosting time is reached.
3. Wrap the joint in foil (shiny side inwards) and rest for the remaining suggested resting time, or until the joint is completely thawed.
4. Proceed to cook as for a fresh joint.

Example

Taking a 1.25-kg/2¾ lb beef topside – frozen

Total defrosting time _____ 16 minutes
Resting time (when defrosting) _____ 60 minutes
Total microwave cooking time _____ 15 minutes
Resting time (when cooking) _____ 35–40 minutes

Following the instructions, place the joint on an upturned plate in a large dish and defrost for four 4-minute periods in the microwave oven, allowing 5-minute resting intervals between each cooking period. Wrap the foil (shiny side inwards) and leave to stand for 45 minutes, or until the joint has defrosted completely.

Unwrap the joint and replace it on the plate then cook in the microwave oven for three periods of 5 minutes, allowing a 5-minute resting interval between each cooking period. Wrap in foil (shiny side inwards) and stand for 25-30 minutes before serving.

Note: Timings will depend on the power ratings of the oven used and the manufacturer's instructions should be consulted.

CHILLI CON CARNI
SERVES 4

1 onion, finely chopped
2 sticks celery
2 carrots, diced
1 green pepper, deseeded and
chopped
1 tablespoon oil
350 g/12 oz minced beef
150 ml/¼ pint tomato juice
150 ml/¼ pint beef stock
1 (227-g/8-oz) can tomatoes
½-1 tablespoon chilli powder,
according to taste
salt and freshly ground black pepper
1 (280-g/10-oz) can kidney beans,
drained
Garnish:
2 tablespoons chopped parsley
(optional)

Place the onion, celery, carrots, pepper and oil in a casserole dish and cook in the microwave for 5 minutes, stirring once. Add the meat and continue to cook in the microwave for 4 minutes. Add all the remaining ingredients, except for the kidney beans, cover and continue to cook for 22 minutes, stirring twice during cooking. Stir in the kidney beans and reheat for 2 minutes. Garnish with chopped parsley.

Variation
Spicy Chilli: If you would like to experiment with the basic chilli recipe, then add 2 tablespoons ground cumin and 1 tablespoon ground coriander to the chilli with the meat. Continue cooking as in the main recipe. The cooked chilli can be topped with 2 rashers lean bacon, chopped and cooked in the microwave for 4 minutes, then served with lots of plain cooked rice (see page 64) or Spicy Turmeric Rice (also on page 64). Alternatively, offer plenty of French bread and a bowl of soured cream with the chilli.

HUNGARIAN BEEF
SERVES 4

*25 g/ 1 oz butter
1 large onion, sliced
2 tablespoons flour
1 (134-g/ 4¾-oz) jar tomato purée
300 ml/½ pint brown stock
1 tablespoon paprika pepper
450 g/ 1 lb topside, cubed
225 g/8 oz tomatoes, skinned
and chopped
salt and freshly ground black pepper*
Garnish:
*2 tablespoons chopped parsley
(optional)*

Melt the butter in a casserole dish in the micro-wave for 1 minute. Add the onion and cook in the microwave for a further 5 minutes. Stir in the flour and gradually add the tomato purée, stock and paprika pepper. Add the meat, stir well and cook in the microwave for 15 minutes, stirring every 2 minutes.

Stir in the tomatoes, cover with foil and leave to stand for 3–5 minutes. Adjust the seasoning before transferring to a heated serving dish. Sprinkle with chopped parsley (if used) and serve with rice, pasta or creamed potatoes. A crisp, fresh green salad makes an excellent accompaniment to this dish.

LAMB IN ONION AND CARAWAY SAUCE
SERVES 4

*50 g/2 oz butter
100 g/4 oz onion, chopped
0.75 kg/ 1½ lb lean lamb (e.g. boned
fillet from leg)
2 tablespoons flour
1 teaspoon tarragon vinegar
1 tablespoon caraway seeds
300 ml/½ pint boiling stock*

Melt the butter in a deep ovenproof dish in the microwave for 1 minute. Add the onion and cook in the microwave for 2 minutes. Cut the lamb into cubes, add to the onion and continue to cook in the microwave for 7 minutes, stirring twice.

Stir in the flour, tarragon vinegar and caraway seeds then carefully add the stock. Season lightly and thicken in the microwave for 10 minutes, stirring 4 times. Taste and adjust seasoning before serving with boiled rice.

Note: Lamb-flavoured stock cubes are available and they are ideal for use in the above recipe. A small bowl of soured cream, sprinkled with chopped chives, would make a welcome accompaniment to both the Lamb in Onion and Caraway Sauce and the Hungarian Beef recipe featured on this page.

Hungarian Beef

STEAK AND KIDNEY PIE

SERVES 4

1 onion, thinly sliced
1 carrot, thinly sliced
25 g/1 oz butter
1 tablespoon oil
450 g/1 lb chuck steak, cubed
100 g/4 oz ox kidney, sliced
seasoned flour
150 ml/¼ pint red wine
300 ml/½ pint beef stock
1 tablespoon Worcestershire sauce
1 bay leaf
mace
salt and freshly ground black pepper
100 g/4 oz button mushrooms
*1 (198-g/7-oz) packet frozen puff
pastry*
1 egg, beaten

Place the onion, butter and oil in a pie dish and cook in the microwave for 4 minutes, stirring once during cooking. Toss the meat and kidney in seasoned flour and add to the onions. Cook in the microwave for 3 minutes. Add all the remaining ingredients except the mushrooms. Cover and cook in the microwave for 20 minutes, stirring frequently. Stand for 5 minutes. Cook in the microwave for a further 13 minutes. Stir in the mushrooms. Allow the meat to cool in the dish before covering with pastry.

To finish the pie, roll out the pastry to an oval shape on a lightly floured board. Cut off a thin border of pastry from the edge and line the rim of the pie dish. Dampen the edges and cover with the pastry. Seal the edges and flute. Make a hole in the centre and brush with beaten egg. Bake in a hot conventional oven (220C, 425F, Gas Mark 7) for 20–30 minutes. Serve with buttered vegetables.

SOMERSET PORK WITH CIDER CREAM SAUCE

SERVES 4

25 g/ 1 oz butter
225 g/ 8 oz onions, chopped
0.75 kg/ 1½ lb pork fillet, trimmed and
cubed
100 g/ 4 oz button mushrooms, sliced
300 ml/½ pint dry cider
salt and freshly ground black pepper
2 tablespoons cornflour
1 tablespoon water
2 tablespoons double cream
Garnish:
chopped parsley

Place the butter in the casserole dish and melt in the microwave for 1 minute. Add the onion and cook for a further 5 minutes. Stir in the cubed pork and cook in the microwave for 8 minutes, stirring 4 times. Add the mushrooms and cider and season lightly. Cook in the microwave for 10 minutes, stirring 4 times. Blend the cornflour with the water, stir into the casserole, then return to the microwave for a further 2 minutes.

Stir the double cream into the sauce and garnish with parsley.

Note: If you prefer the meat to be browner, seal the pork under a preheated grill before cooking in the microwave. The timing will be slightly reduced if this method is chosen.

PORK CASSEROLE WITH APPLE

SERVES 4

25 g/ 1 oz butter
1 large onion, quartered
1 tablespoon flour
0.75 kg/ 1½ lb lean pork, cut in
bite-size pieces
few sprigs mixed fresh herbs,
tied in a bundle
175 ml/ 6 fl oz dry white wine
salt and freshly ground black pepper
1 large green-skinned eating apple,
cored and sliced
juice of ½ lemon
50 g/ 2 oz mushrooms, sliced

Cook the butter and onion in a casserole dish in the microwave for 8 minutes. Stir in the flour, add the meat and herbs and carefully stir in the wine. Season lightly and cook in the microwave for 7 minutes, stirring 3 times.

Dip the apple slices in the lemon juice to prevent discoloration and add to the casserole together with the mushrooms. Cook in the microwave for 5 minutes, stirring once during cooking. Remove the herbs from the casserole before serving.

Note: Fresh or canned fruit can be used to enhance the rich flavour of pork. Canned apricots, peaches or pineapple can be used instead of the apple in the above recipe.

Vegetable Dishes

Vegetable	Quantity or Weight	Cooking utensil	Quantity of water or butter used	Microwave cooking time 6.00 W
Artichokes, globe	1 medium	cook-bag	4 tablespoons water	8–10 minutes
Artichokes, jerusalem	450 g/1 lb peeled	cook-bag	2 tablespoons lemon juice, 25 g/1 oz butter	10–12 minutes
Asparagus	450 g/1 lb medium spears, trimmed	cook-bag	2 tablespoons water	5–7 minutes
Beans, broad	450 g/1 lb (shelled weight)	cook-bag	2 tablespoons water	5–7 minutes
Beans, French	450 g/1 lb	cook-bag	3 tablespoons water	7–8 minutes
Beans, runner	450 g/1 lb sliced	cook-bag	3 tablespoons water	5–7 minutes
Beetroot	4 medium	cook-bag	4 tablespoons water	10 minutes
Broccoli	450 g/1 lb	cook-bag	3 tablespoons water	7–8 minutes
Cabbage	450 g/1 lb shredded	cook-bag	2 tablespoons water	10 minutes
Carrots	225 g/8 oz in 1-cm/½-inch slices	cook-bag	2 tablespoons water	5 minutes

Vegetable	Quantity or Weight	Cooking utensil	Quantity of water or butter used	Microwave cooking time 600W
Cauliflower	225 g/8 oz broken in florets	cook-bag	4 tablespoons water	5 minutes
Corn on the cob	2 cobs with husks removed	cook-bag	3 tablespoons water	8–10 minutes
Courgettes	450 g/1 lb sliced	cook-bag	25 g/1 oz butter	3 minutes plus 10 minutes standing time
Leeks	450 g/1 lb sliced	cook-bag	25 g/1 oz butter	5–7 minutes
Mushrooms, button	225 g/8 oz whole	cook-bag	25 g/1 oz butter	$1\frac{1}{2}$ minutes
Onions, whole	175 g/6 oz each (2 at a time)	cook-bag	2 tablespoons water	10 minutes
Parsnips	450 g/1 lb sliced	cook-bag	2 tablespoons water	10 minutes
Peas	450 g/1 lb (shelled weight)	cook-bag	2 tablespoons water	8 minutes
Potatoes, baked	1 kg/2 lb (4 large even-sized)	on kitchen paper	—	18–20 minutes
Potatoes, boiled	450 g/1 lb (in 50-g/2-oz pieces)	cook-bag	3 tablespoons water	5–7 minutes
Potatoes, new	450 g/1 lb (even-sized)	cook-bag	4 tablespoons water	5 minutes
Spinach	450 g/1 lb	cook-bag	—	5–6 minutes
Spring greens	450 g/1 lb	cook-bag	—	8 minutes
Swede	450 g/1 lb (in 25-g/1-oz pieces)	cook-bag	2 tablespoons water	10 minutes

ASPARAGUS IN LEMON BUTTER

SERVES 4

450 g/ 1 lb asparagus
2 tablespoons hot water
100 g/4 oz butter
juice of $\frac{1}{2}$ lemon
salt and freshly ground black pepper
grated Parmesan cheese (optional)

Trim off all the white woody part of the asparagus to give even-length spears weighing approximately 350 g/12 oz.

Lay the spears flat in the cook-bag, making sure that the trimmed ends do not overlap. Spoon the water into the bag and seal loosely with an elastic band. Cook in the microwave for 5–7 minutes. Carefully open the bag and test the asparagus with a knife. The cooking time may vary a little depending on the thickness and age of the asparagus.

Place the butter and lemon juice in a pudding basin and season well. Melt in the microwave for 5 minutes and pour over the asparagus before serving. Sprinkle with a little parmesan cheese, if liked.

Variations

Asparagus with prawns: This is excellent to serve as a starter or for a light lunch. Add 225–350 g/8–12 oz peeled cooked prawns to the butter and lemon juice. Increase the time for melting the butter to about 7–10 minutes, depending on the quantity of prawns used. Spoon the buttered prawns over the asparagus and serve at once, with thinly sliced wholemeal bread and butter.

Mimosa asparagus: Cook the asparagus as above and prepare the butter to pour over it. Omit the Parmesan cheese but top the asparagus with finely chopped hard-boiled eggs and chopped parsley. Serve with thin pieces of dark rye bread.

Asparagus in Lemon Butter

CAULIFLOWER CHEESE

SERVES 4

I cauliflower
4 tablespoons water
I quantity Cheese sauce (page 53)
50 g/2 oz Cheddar cheese, grated
25 g/1 oz fresh breadcrumbs
(optional)

Trim the outer stalks off the cauliflower and wash it thoroughly. Shake off all the washing water, then put the cauliflower in a cook-bag and sprinkle in the measured water. Secure the end loosely with an elastic band and cook in the microwave for 7–10 minutes. The cooking time will vary slightly according to the size of the vegetable. Turn the cauliflower over and around once during cooking.

Leave the cauliflower in the bag with the end closed tightly while you make the sauce.

Open the bag and transfer the cauliflower, drained of all water, to a flameproof serving dish. Pour the sauce over the cauliflower. Mix the cheese with the breadcrumbs, if used, and sprinkle over the sauce. Brown the top under a hot grill.

Cauliflower Cheese

COURGETTES À LA GREQUE

SERVES 4

2 tablespoons oil
25 g/1 oz butter
0.5 kg/1 lb courgettes, sliced
2 cloves garlic, crushed
4 tomatoes, skinned and sliced
100 g/4 oz button mushrooms
Garnish:
chopped parsley

Place the oil and butter in an oval dish and melt in the microwave for 1 minute. Add the courgettes and garlic and mix well. Cover with cling film and cook in the microwave for 2 minutes. Stir in the tomatoes and mushrooms, cover and cook in the microwave for a further 2 minutes. Stir the vegetables thoroughly, bringing the outside vegetables to the centre of the dish and vice versa. Cover and continue to cook in the microwave for a further 2 minutes. Allow to cool slightly before serving. Garnish with chopped parsley.

STUFFED BAKED POTATOES

SERVES 4

4 large potatoes, about 225 g/8 oz each

Prick the skins of the potatoes and place as far apart as possible on a double thickness of kitchen paper in the microwave oven. Cook for 18–20 minutes, depending on the size of the potatoes, re-arranging 4 times during cooking.

Halve the potatoes and top with any of the following fillings:

CURRIED PRAWN

25 g/1 oz butter
2 teaspoons curry powder
50 g/2 oz onion, chopped
2 tablespoons flour
150 ml/¼ pint milk
225 g/8 oz peeled prawns
salt and freshly ground black pepper

In a soufflé dish melt the butter in the microwave for 1 minute. Add the curry powder and onion and cook in the microwave for 5 minutes. Add the flour and mix to a smooth sauce with the milk. Stir in the prawns and continue to cook in the microwave for 5 minutes. Season.

APPLE AND FRANKFURTER

50 g/2 oz onion, grated
1 large eating apple, chopped
1 (170-g/6-oz) packet frankfurters,
cut in chunks
¼ teaspoon sage
2 teaspoons cornflour
3 tablespoons water
2 tablespoons double cream
salt and freshly ground black pepper

In a soufflé dish mix together the onion, apple, frankfurters and sage. Stir well and cook in the microwave for 2 minutes. Blend the cornflour with the water, add the cream and pour over the other ingredients. Heat in the microwave for a further 2 minutes, stirring twice. Taste and season.

CREAMED AVOCADO

2 ripe avocado pears
1 tablespoon lemon juice
2 tablespoons double cream
freshly ground black pepper
chopped chives

Halve the pears, remove the stones, and cream the flesh with the lemon juice and cream. Season with freshly ground black pepper and pile on top of the halved potatoes. Sprinkle with chopped chives before serving.

CELERY AND CREAM CHEESE

225 g/8 oz cream cheese
3 sticks celery, finely chopped
freshly ground black pepper

Mix together the cream cheese and celery, season with pepper and pile on to the halved potatoes immediately before serving.

LEEKS IN CREAMY WINE SAUCE

SERVES 4

0.75 kg/1½ lb leeks, washed
and trimmed
150 ml/¼ pint dry white wine
150 ml/¼ pint boiling chicken stock
3 teaspoons cornflour
3 tablespoons double cream
salt and freshly ground black pepper

Slice the leeks and place in a cook-bag with the wine. Seal loosely with an elastic band and cook in the microwave for 6 minutes.

Strain the leeks, reserving the cooking liquid, and place in a serving dish. Pour the cooking liquid into a measuring jug together with the stock. Blend the cornflour with the cream and stir into the stock. Season and thicken in the microwave for 3 minutes, stirring twice during cooking. Pour over the leeks before serving.

STUFFED CABBAGE LEAVES

SERVES 4

8 large cabbage leaves
1.75 litres/3 pints hot water
Stuffing:
225 g/8 oz garlic sausage, chopped
50 g/2 oz button mushrooms, chopped
2 tablespoons grated onion
4 tablespoons fresh brown
breadcrumbs
1 egg, beaten
salt and finely ground black pepper
Sauce:
1 (396-g/14-oz) can tomatoes
1 bay leaf
½ teaspoon dried mixed herbs
1 beef stock cube, crumbled
2 tablespoons tomato purée
2 teaspoons cornflour

Place the cabbage leaves in a large mixing bowl with the hot water and blanch in the microwave for 3 minutes until they are just cooked. Drain well. In a smaller mixing bowl mix together the ingredients for the stuffing and season lightly. Cook in the microwave for 3 minutes, stirring once.

Divide the stuffing between the cabbage leaves and carefully roll up, folding in the sides of the leaves to form small parcels. Carefully place them in the cook-bag, loosely seal with an elastic band and heat in the microwave for 1 minute, immediately before serving.

Place all the ingredients for the sauce, except the cornflour, in the measuring jug and cook in the microwave for 5 minutes. Strain off the liquid and reserve. Return the sauce to the jug. Blend the cornflour with a little of the reserved liquid and stir into the sauce. In the microwave thicken the sauce for 2 minutes, stirring once, and serve poured over the cabbage leaves.

TUNA-STUFFED PEPPERS

SERVES 4

100 g/4 oz long grain rice
300 ml/½ pint hand hot water (about
48 C/120 F)
½ teaspoon salt
4 green or red peppers (about 75 g/
3 oz each)
50 g/2 oz onion, chopped
25 g/1 oz butter
1 (198-g/7-oz) can tuna, drained
1 tablespoon lemon juice
100 g/4 oz cucumber, peeled and
chopped
50 g/2 oz mature Cheddar cheese,
finely grated
salt and freshly ground black pepper

In a measuring jug, mix the rice with the water and salt and cook in the microwave for 10 minutes. Cut the tops off the peppers and remove the seeds and pith from the insides. In a pudding basin, mix the onion and butter and cook in the microwave for 2 minutes. Add the fish, lemon juice, cucumber and cheese. Stir in the cooked rice and season to taste. Pile this mixture into the peppers and place them in a round shallow dish. Pour 150 ml/¼ pint hand hot water in the dish and cook in the microwave for 12 minutes. Serve with a tomato sauce (see page 54), if liked.

Sauces

Sauces cooked in the microwave are always foolproof. No more burnt saucepans to wash up!
It is, however, important to make sure that the bowl, basin or jug in which you cook the sauce is big enough to avoid having any sauces boiling over in the oven. If the sauce boat is suitable for microwave cooking, then you can make and serve the sauce in it.
Most of these sauces can be made in advance and then reheated in the microwave just before serving. It really is worthwhile taking the trouble to make a sauce as it can add that special finishing touch to a dish.

WHITE SAUCE WITH VARIATIONS

MAKES 300 ml /½ pint

25 g/ I oz butter
25 g/ I oz flour
300 ml/½ pint milk
salt and freshly ground black pepper

Melt the butter in a measuring jug in the microwave for I minute. Stir in the flour until well mixed then pour in the milk and stir well. Cook in the microwave for 4 minutes, stirring after every minute to prevent lumps forming. Season to taste.

Variations
Cheese sauce: Stir 50 g/2 oz grated cheese into the cooked sauce.
Anchovy sauce: Add I–2 tablespoons anchovy essence to the cooked sauce.
Parsley sauce: Stir 2–3 tablespoons chopped parsley into the cooked sauce.
Mushroom sauce: Stir 50 g/2 oz chopped cooked mushrooms into the cooked sauce.

TOMATO SAUCE

MAKES 450ml /¾ pint

15 g/½ oz butter
1 small onion, finely chopped
25 g/1 oz flour
1 (396-g/14-oz) can tomatoes
pinch basil
few drops Worcestershire sauce
salt and freshly ground black pepper
150 ml/¼ pint red wine
1 chicken stock cube, crumbled
2 tablespoons tomato purée
1 tablespoon chopped parsley
(optional)

Place the butter and chopped onion in a pudding basin and cook in the microwave for 2 minutes, stirring once during cooking. Stir in the flour, then add the remaining ingredients. Return to the microwave for 5 minutes, stirring twice. Allow to cool slightly before liquidizing. Reheat in the microwave if necessary.

BREAD SAUCE

MAKES 300ml /½ pint

1 small onion, studded with 6 cloves
300 ml/½ pint milk
75 g/3 oz fresh breadcrumbs
25 g/1 oz butter

Place the onion and the milk in a large measuring jug and cook in the microwave for 4 minutes. Remove the onion and stir in the breadcrumbs and butter. Stand for 30 minutes. Reheat in the microwave for 1–2 minutes. Serve bread sauce with game and poultry dishes, especially with the Christmas turkey.

CUMBERLAND SAUCE

MAKES 450ml /¾ pint

2 tablespoons soft brown sugar
pinch cayenne pepper
150 ml/¼ pint hot chicken stock, made
with a stock cube
150 ml/¼ pint red wine
1 tablespoon cornflour
3 tablespoons redcurrant jelly
grated rind of ½ small orange
2 tablespoons orange juice
salt and freshly ground black pepper

Place the sugar, cayenne, chicken stock and wine in a pudding basin and cook in the microwave for 3 minutes. Blend the cornflour with a little cold water and stir into the sauce. Add the remaining ingredients and continue to cook in the microwave for 2 minutes. This sauce makes an excellent accompaniment to gammon or pork dishes.

APPLE SAUCE

MAKES 300ml /½ pint

450 g/1 lb cooking apples, peeled,
cored and sliced
2 tablespoons water
25 g/1 oz butter

Place all the ingredients in a pudding basin and cook in the microwave for 2½ minutes, stirring once during cooking. Sieve or mash the sauce until smooth. Serve with pork dishes and roast duck.

Tomato Sauce and Cumberland Sauce

SWEET 'N' SOUR SAUCE

MAKES 750ml / 1¼ pints

2 tablespoons oil
100g/4oz onion, coarsely chopped
100g/4oz green pepper, coarsely chopped
100g/4oz carrots, cut into strips
6 tablespoons tomato ketchup
2 tablespoons soy sauce
3 tablespoons dry sherry
2 tablespoons wine vinegar
1 (226-g/8-oz) can pineapple chunks
1 tablespoon brown sugar

Heat the oil in a mixing bowl in the microwave for 2 minutes then add the onion, pepper and carrot and continue to cook in the microwave for a further 5 minutes. Stir in all the remaining ingredients and cook in the microwave for a further 5 minutes.

Serve this tangy sauce with cooked pork, lamb, poultry or fish.

Sweet 'n' Sour Sauce

HOLLANDAISE SAUCE

MAKES ABOUT 300ml/½pint

2 tablespoons lemon juice
1 tablespoon water
salt and freshly ground white pepper
100g/4oz butter
2 large egg yolks

Pour the lemon juice and water into a 1.15-litre/2-pint basin (you need one this size for room to whisk vigorously later). Add a little seasoning and cook on full power for 6 minutes.

Meanwhile place the butter in a heatproof measuring jug or small basin. When the lemon juice is removed from the oven whisk in the egg yolks immediately. Heat the butter for 2½ minutes, then slowly pour it on to the egg yolks whisking continuously.

Cook the hollandaise sauce for 30 seconds, give it a good stir and serve at once.

BRANDY SAUCE
MAKES 300 ml /½ pint

25 g/ 1 oz cornflour
300 ml/½ pint milk
25 g/ 1 oz caster sugar
15 g/½ oz butter
1 tablespoon brandy

Blend the cornflour with a little of the milk until smooth. Place the remaining milk in a measuring jug and heat in the microwave for 1 minute. Pour on to the blended cornflour and then return to the jug. Cook in the microwave for 1½ minutes, whisking after 1 minute. Add the sugar, butter and brandy, and whisk until smooth.

CHOCOLATE SAUCE
MAKES 300 ml /½ pint

100 g/4 oz plain cooking chocolate
5 tablespoons golden syrup
3 tablespoons cocoa powder
3 tablespoons warm water
1 oz butter, melted

Place the chocolate, broken into pieces, with the syrup in a pudding basin, and melt in the microwave for 2 minutes. In a separate basin, blend the cocoa powder with the water and butter. Add to the chocolate mixture and cook in the microwave for a further 30 seconds.

CUSTARD SAUCE
MAKES 300 ml /½ pint

300 ml/½ pint milk
2 eggs
4 tablespoons caster sugar
few drops vanilla essence

Heat the milk in a measuring jug in the microwave for 3 minutes, or until just boiling. Lightly whisk the eggs, sugar and essence. Pour the milk on to the whisked mixture, mix well and strain back into the jug. Return to the microwave for 4 minutes, standing the jug in a water-bath of hand-hot tap water, stirring every minute. The custard should lightly coat the back of a spoon when cooked.

HOT BARBECUE SAUCE
MAKES 200 ml / 7 fl oz

1 small onion, grated
4 tablespoons tomato purée
150 ml/¼ pint water
1 tablespoon wine vinegar
1 tablespoon Worcestershire sauce
2 teaspoons brown sugar
salt and freshly ground black pepper
2 tablespoons redcurrant jelly

Place all the ingredients together in a basin and cook in the microwave for 9 minutes, stirring 3 times during cooking. This sauce is delicious served with pork or lamb.

CURRY SAUCE
MAKES 450 ml /¾ pint

1 onion, finely chopped
1 clove garlic, crushed
25 g/ 1 oz butter
1 tablespoon oil
3 tablespoons curry powder
1 tablespoon flour
2 tablespoons tomato purée
pinch ground cloves
2 tablespoons chutney
pinch cayenne pepper
salt and freshly ground black pepper
1 teaspoon lemon juice
1 teaspoon black treacle
450 ml/¾ pint hot chicken stock
few drops Worcestershire sauce

Place the onion, garlic, butter and oil in a basin and cook in the microwave for 4 minutes, stirring twice during the cooking time. Stir in the remaining ingredients and continue to cook in the microwave for 10 minutes, stirring frequently. Serve with meat, fish or egg dishes.

Egg & Cheese Dishes

Egg and cheese dishes cook particularly well in the microwave oven. Most of the recipes in this chapter take 10 minutes or less to cook. There are two important points to remember when cooking eggs in the microwave. Firstly, you cannot boil eggs in their shells as they will burst, and secondly, foods that are egged and breadcrumbed become leathery. Care must be taken not to overcook egg and cheese dishes as they can quickly become indigestible.

CHEESE FONDUE

SERVES 4

1 clove garlic
150 ml/¼ pint white wine
1 teaspoon lemon juice
450 g/1 lb Gruyère or
Emmenthal cheese, grated
1 tablespoon cornflour
2 tablespoons brandy
pinch freshly ground nutmeg
freshly ground black pepper

Cut the clove of garlic in half and rub the cut sides around the inside of a fondue dish. Pour in the wine and lemon juice and heat in the microwave for 1–2 minutes until just hot. Stir in a third of the cheese, heat in the microwave for 1 minute then repeat with the remaining two-thirds of cheese, adding a third at a time and cook in the microwave for 1 minute in between. After the final amount of cheese has been added return to the microwave for 1 minute, stirring after 30 seconds. Blend the cornflour with the brandy and stir into the fondue. Season to taste and return to the microwave for 2 minutes, stirring frequently. Cool slightly before serving, with cubes of French bread, celery or florets of cauliflower to dip.

STILTON BAKED EGGS

SERVES 4

1 (170-g/6-oz) packet frozen chopped
spinach, thawed
100 g/4 oz Stilton cheese, crumbled
4 standard eggs
little grated nutmeg

Divide the spinach between 4 ramekin dishes. Reserve a little of the Stilton cheese and sprinkle the rest on top of the spinach in the ramekins. Break an egg in each dish and sprinkle with a little nutmeg. Sprinkle the remaining cheese over the eggs and cook two at a time in the microwave for 1½ minutes, checking the eggs after 1 minute. Serve hot with Melba toast.

Note: When cooking eggs in the microwave oven, the timing is particularly critical as the eggs should be removed before they are completely cooked.

BAKED VIENNA EGGS

SERVES 4

4 crisp Vienna rolls
4 short rashers bacon
4 standard eggs
salt and freshly ground black pepper

Cut the top of each roll and hollow out the soft bread from the centre. Line each roll with a rasher of bacon and crack an egg into the cavity. Season lightly and place 2 rolls on a plate. Cook 2 rolls at a time in the microwave for 2 minutes to 2 minutes 15 seconds depending on how well cooked the egg is liked.

Note: The bread scooped out from the rolls may be made into breadcrumbs and dried or frozen for later use.

SCRAMBLED EGGS SUPREME

SERVES 4

6 eggs
50 g/2 oz button mushrooms, chopped
25 g/1 oz cheese, grated
75 g/3 oz garlic sausage, chopped
3 tablespoons double cream
salt and freshly ground black pepper

Whisk the eggs in the pudding basin, add the mushrooms and cook in the microwave for 1 minute, stirring once.

Add the cheese, garlic sausage and cream, season lightly and return to the microwave for 3 minutes, stirring every minute, until almost set. Stir well and leave for 1 minute before serving with hot buttered toast.

Scrambled Eggs Supreme

CHEESY FLOWERPOT LOAVES

MAKES 6

175 g/6 oz wholewheat flour
25 g/1 oz wheat bran
½ teaspoon salt
½ teaspoon dry mustard
50 g/2 oz Farmhouse English Cheddar
cheese, finely grated
1½ teaspoons dried yeast
1 teaspoon sugar
300 ml/½ pint tepid water
1 egg, beaten

Place a small round of greaseproof paper in the base of 6, 7.5-cm/3-inch clay flowerpots to cover the hole. In a mixing bowl, mix together the wholewheat flour, bran, salt, mustard and cheese. Dissolve the dried yeast with the sugar in the water and leave in a warm place until it becomes frothy, then whisk in the beaten egg.

Mix the yeast liquid into the dry ingredients and beat well to form a soft mixture. Divide the mixture between the 6 flowerpots and cover with a piece of polythene or cling film. Leave in a warm place until the mixture has almost doubled in size.

Uncover the pots and cook in the microwave two at a time, allowing 3 minutes for each pair. When cooked, slide a knife between the bread and the flowerpot and turn out on to a wire rack to cool. Remove the greaseproof paper from the base of the breads. Serve with butter and cheese or instead of conventional rolls.

Note: These are best eaten on the day they are made.

Variations

Herby cheese flowerpot loaves: Add 2 teaspoons dried mixed herbs to the dry ingredients, then proceed as for the basic recipe.
Nutty cheese flowerpot loaves: Add 50 g/2 oz chopped walnuts to the dry ingredients, then proceed as for the basic recipe.
Cheesy fruit flowerpot loaves: Add 50 g/2 oz sultanas to the dry ingredients, then proceed as for the basic recipe.

Cheesy Flowerpot Loaves

POTATO PIZZA

SERVES 4

350 g/12 oz mashed potato
25 g/1 oz fine dried white
breadcrumbs
1 teaspoon dried mixed herbs
salt and freshly ground black pepper
100 g/4 oz onion, chopped
50 g/2 oz green pepper, chopped
100 g/4 oz streaky bacon, chopped
1 (396-g/14-oz) can tomatoes, drained
175 g/6 oz cheese, grated
1 (50-g/1¾-oz) can anchovy fillets
few black olives

Mix together the mashed potato, breadcrumbs and herbs. Season lightly and press in the base and slightly up the sides of a round shallow dish.

Mix together the onion, green pepper and bacon in a pudding basin and cook in the microwave for 5 minutes. Arrange this mixture on the potato base. Top with the drained tomatoes and grated cheese. Arrange the anchovy fillets in a lattice pattern on top of the pizza and cook in the microwave for 4 minutes, turning the dish 4 times during cooking. Place an olive in each square of the lattice before serving.

Note: A wide variety of ingredients can be added to, or substituted in, the above recipe. Canned tuna fish, peeled cooked prawns, chopped cooked ham or chicken, sliced or chopped salami or garlic sausage, capers, canned artichoke hearts or sliced mushrooms are all suitable additions.

MIXED VEGETABLES AU GRATIN

SERVES 4–6

350 g/12 oz cauliflower florets
2 tablespoons water
1 large onion, thinly sliced
1 large green pepper, cut in rings
25 g/1 oz butter
2 medium beetroot, cooked and
chopped
salt and freshly ground black pepper
150 ml/¼ pint double cream
¼ teaspoon lemon juice
1 clove garlic, crushed
100 g/4 oz mature Cheddar cheese,
grated
50 g/2 oz fresh brown breadcrumbs
2 hard-boiled eggs, chopped
1 tablespoon chopped parsley

Place the cauliflower and water in the cook-bag, secure the end loosely with an elastic band and cook in the microwave for 5 minutes. Remove the cauliflower to a strainer and place the onion and green pepper in the bag with the butter. Secure the end with the elastic band, again allowing room for the steam to escape, and cook in the microwave for 8 minutes. Shake the bag twice during cooking.

Place the beetroot in the bottom of the oblong dish and arrange the onion and pepper on top, pouring over the butter from the cook-bag. Place the cauliflower florets on top and season well.

Mix the cream and lemon juice, add the garlic and pour evenly over the vegetables. Mix together the cheese and breadcrumbs and sprinkle over the top of the dish. Cook in the microwave for 6 minutes, turning the dish 3 times during cooking. Mix together the chopped hard-boiled eggs and parsley and spoon this down the middle of the dish. Serve hot or cold.

MACARONI CHEESE DE LUXE

SERVES 4

*225 g / 8 oz macaroni, broken into
short lengths
generous litre / 2 pints hot water
1 teaspoon salt
50 g / 2 oz butter
150 g / 5 oz onion, finely chopped
25 g / 1 oz flour
600 ml / 1 pint milk
175 g / 6 oz Cheddar cheese, grated
salt and freshly ground black pepper
paprika pepper (optional)*
Garnish:
*2 tomatoes, sliced
chopped parsley*

Place the macaroni in a large mixing bowl with the water and salt. Cook in the microwave for 15 minutes, stirring twice during cooking; drain and rinse.

Melt the butter in a smaller mixing bowl in the microwave for 1 minute, then add the onion and continue to cook in the microwave for 6 minutes. Stir in the flour to absorb the butter, then gradually mix in the milk. Add the grated cheese and cook in the microwave for 5 minutes, stirring twice during cooking.

Add the macaroni, season lightly and return to the microwave for 4 minutes, stirring 4 times during cooking.

Transfer to a serving dish, sprinkle with paprika and garnish with tomato slices and parsley before serving.

Rice & Pasta

Rice and pasta can be cooked quickly and easily in the microwave oven, using the normal proportions of liquid. Fill the cooking vessel only half to three-quarters full for successful results. Small amounts of rice (100 g/4 oz, for example) are successfully cooked in a 600-ml/1-pint measuring jug. The shape of the jug helps rapid cooking.

Cooked rice freezes well and it can be rapidly defrosted in the microwave. For best results the rice should be frozen in a cook-bag which can be removed from the freezer, punctured and then, discarding any metal clips, placed in the microwave oven to be reheated to serving temperature within minutes.

The type of rice used may alter the cooking time. Most successful are the long-grain varieties which cook by the absorption method. Brown rice can be quickly and successfully cooked in the microwave.

RICE SALAD

SERVES 4–6

BASIC RICE

225 g/8 oz long-grain rice
600 ml/1 pint hot water (about 65C/150F)
1 teaspoon salt

Place all the ingredients in a basin and cook in the microwave for 15 minutes, stirring 3 times.

SPICY TURMERIC RICE

100 g/4 oz long-grain rice
300 ml/½ pint hot water (about 65C/150F)
¼ teaspoon turmeric
½ teaspoon salt

Place all the ingredients in a measuring jug and cook in the microwave for 10 minutes, stirring halfway through the cooking time.

VEGETABLES

sliced courgettes, red cabbage, shredded endive, tomato slices, watercress, shredded white cabbage, peas, grated carrot, cress, sliced aubergine and radishes
Garnish:
sliced hard-boiled egg
soured cream
chopped parsley

Serve the cold rice on a large platter, alternating with a selection of prepared vegetables. Garnish with slices of hard-boiled egg and serve with soured cream sprinkled with parsley.

MUSSEL PAELLA

SERVES 4

1 small onion, finely chopped
½ green or red pepper, cut into fine strips
1 tablespoon oil
¼ teaspoon turmeric
225 g/8 oz long-grain rice
600 ml/1 pint hot chicken stock
2 tablespoons chopped parsley
1 tablespoon chopped chives
salt and freshly ground black pepper
2 (150-g/5¼-oz) cans mussels, drained
3 tomatoes, skinned and chopped

Place the onion, pepper and oil in an oval dish and cook in the microwave for 5 minutes, stirring once during cooking.

Stir in the turmeric, rice, chicken stock, parsley, chives and seasoning. Cook in the microwave for a further 10 minutes, stirring after 5 minutes. Add the mussels and tomatoes and heat in the microwave for a further 4 minutes. Remove to a heated serving dish, if liked.

Note: A selection of seafood, cubed cooked chicken and vegetables can be added to the paella, as shown below.

Peeled cooked prawns: Add 100 g/4 oz peeled cooked prawns (defrosted if frozen) with the mussels in the above recipe. Whole cooked prawns can be used to garnish the paella.

Fresh mussels: Leave fresh mussels overnight in cold water with a handful of oatmeal added. Scrub and remove their beards, discard any open ones, then place in a mixing bowl with 150 ml/¼ pint of water and seasoning to taste. Cover with cling film and cook for 5 minutes, stirring once. Remove from the shells, discarding any which have not opened and reserve a few for garnish. Add to the paella instead of bottled mussels.

Vegetables: Thinly sliced carrots and frozen peas can be added to the paella with the rice.

CREAMED NOODLES WITH MUSHROOMS

SERVES 4

175 g/6 oz ribbon noodles
¼ teaspoon salt
450 ml/¾ pint boiling water
100 g/4 oz button mushrooms
15 g/½ oz butter
salt and freshly ground black pepper
150 ml/¼ pint double cream
Garnish:
poppy seeds
chopped parsley

Place the noodles, salt and boiling water in a small round dish, cover with cling film and cook in the microwave for 5 minutes, stirring after 3 minutes. Drain and rinse under hot water.

Place the mushrooms and butter in a larger dish and cook in the microwave for 1 minute. Stir in the noodles, seasoning and cream. Heat in the microwave for 2 minutes, stirring once. Garnish with poppy seeds and chopped parsley.

Variations

Noodles with Ham: Add 100 g/4 oz cooked ham, cut into fine strips, to the noodles and heat for about 4 minutes.

Noodles with Prawns: Add 225 g/8 oz peeled cooked prawns to the noodles with the cream. Stir in the grated rind of 1 lemon if you like and add 1 tablespoon choppd chives. Heat through as above, allowing a few minutes extra.

Noodles with Pine Nuts and Basil: Prepare the noodles as in the main recipe. Add 3 table-spoons pine nuts and 2 tablespoons chopped fresh basil with the cream and heat through, allowing just a little extra time. Omit the poppy seeds and chopped parsley.

Noodles with Salami and Spring Onions: Add 100 g/4 oz finely shredded salami and 1 bunch chopped spring onions to the noodles with the cream. Heat through as above, allowing a little extra time. Omit the poppy seeds and parsley.

STUFFED CANNELLONI

SERVES 4

1 small onion, finely chopped
1 tablespoon oil
175 g/6 oz chicken livers
175-g/8-oz can tomatoes
225 g/8 oz mushrooms, finely chopped
8 tubes cannelloni
900 ml/1½ pints boiling water
Tomato Sauce (see page 54)
grated Parmesan cheese

Place the onion and oil in an oblong pie dish and cook in the microwave for 3–4 minutes, until the onion is soft. Stir in the chicken livers and continue to cook in the microwave for 3 minutes, stirring once. Add the tomatoes and mushrooms and cook in the microwave for a further 2 minutes.

Place the cannelloni tubes in an oval dish and pour over the boiling water, making sure the cannelloni is immersed. Cook in the microwave for 10 minutes, stopping half way through the cooking time to rearrange the cannelloni. Drain and stuff each tube with the filling, using a teaspoon. Return the cannelloni to the oval dish. Pour over the tomato sauce, making sure the cannelloni is covered. Sprinkle with Parmesan cheese and reheat in the microwave for 1 minute.

SPAGHETTI BOLOGNESE

SERVES 4

225 g/8 oz short-cut spaghetti
generous litre/2 pints boiling water
1 teaspoon salt
25 g/1 oz butter
225 g/8 oz onion, chopped
1 green pepper, chopped
100 g/4 oz mushrooms, sliced
450 g/1 lb minced beef
1 clove garlic, crushed
1 (397-g/14-oz) can tomatoes
2 tablespoons tomato purée
150 ml/¼ pint hot beef stock
grated Parmesan cheese (optional)

Place the spaghetti in an oblong dish and pour over the boiling water. Add the salt and cook in the microwave for 15 minutes. Leave to stand in the water for 10 minutes before draining and rinsing in boiling water.

Place the butter, together with the onion and green pepper, in a mixing bowl and cook in the microwave for 5 minutes, stirring twice during cooking. Add the mushrooms, minced beef and garlic. Mix together well before stirring in the tomatoes, tomato purée and stock. Cook in the microwave for a further 15 minutes, stirring every 2 minutes. Serve the meat sauce on the spaghetti and sprinkle with a little Parmesan cheese, if liked.

Puddings & Desserts

In this chapter the microwave oven shows just how versatile it can be. Whether you want ice cream, cheesecake or Christmas pudding for dessert, there is something for every taste. Christmas puddings are no longer the trial they used to be, as the microwave will cook a pudding in only 9 minutes!

CRUNCHY APPLE CRISP

SERVES 4

3 cooking apples peeled, cored and sliced
4 tablespoons undiluted orange juice, thawed
75 g/3 oz brown sugar
50 g/2 oz butter, softened
175 g/6 oz plain sweet biscuits, crushed
Garnish:
orange slices

Place the apples evenly on the base of a flan dish and spoon over the orange juice.

Lightly mix together the sugar, butter and crushed biscuits and spoon over the apples. Cook in the microwave for 5–7 minutes, until the apples are soft. Garnish with orange slices and serve hot with cream.

Note: To thaw frozen orange juice in the microwave, place the frozen juice in a 300-ml/½-pint glass measuring jug and place in the microwave for 1 minute. Stir well.

PINEAPPLE AND ORANGE TURNABOUT

SERVES 4

1 (226-g/8-oz) can pineapple slices, drained
glacé cherries
4 tablespoons undiluted orange juice, thawed
110 g/4 oz soft margarine
110 g/4 oz caster sugar
2 eggs
110 g/4 oz self-raising flour
Decoration:
150 ml/¼ pint double cream, whipped
angelica

Line a dish with cling film and arrange the pineapple slices decoratively on the base. Place a glacé cherry half in the centre of each slice and pour over the orange juice. Place the remaining ingredients in a mixing bowl and beat until well mixed. Spoon over the pineapple, spreading evenly. Cook in the microwave for 10–12 minutes, giving the dish a half turn after the first 5 minutes. Turn out on to a plate and decorate with rosettes of whipped cream and angelica.

CHRISTMAS PUDDING

SERVES 4–6

75 g/3 oz butter
175 g/6 oz currants
100 g/4 oz raisins
100 g/4 oz sultanas
25 g/1 oz dried apricots, chopped
15 g/½ oz almonds, chopped
75 g/3 oz plain flour
pinch mixed spice
pinch nutmeg
75 g/3 oz soft dark brown sugar
2 eggs
rind and juice of 1 lemon
2 tablespoons black treacle
grated rind of 1 orange
1 tablespoon brandy
gravy browning to colour (optional)

Place all the ingredients in a mixing bowl and mix well together. Add a few drops of gravy browning if a dark pudding is preferred. Place in a lightly-greased pudding basin and cover with greased greaseproof paper, securing with an elastic band around the rim. Cook in the microwave for 5 minutes, then allow to stand for 5 minutes. Cook in the microwave for a further 3 minutes and stand for 5 minutes. Finally cook for 1 minute and allow to stand for a few minutes before turning out. Serve hot with Brandy Sauce (see page 57).

To flame the pudding, warm 2 tablespoons brandy for a few seconds in the microwave. Pour over the pudding and ignite. Serve at once.

If keeping the pudding, loosely cover with cling film to prevent the surface hardening. When cold, wrap in the greaseproof paper and foil, and place in an airtight container.

Note: This pudding will keep for up to 2 months. Do not add the traditional coin to a microwave Christmas pudding.

BANANA BAKE

SERVES 4

4 bananas, peeled
4 tablespoons undiluted orange juice,
thawed
6 tablespoons white wine
1 tablespoon lemon juice
50 g/2 oz brown sugar

Slice the bananas in half lengthways, then cut each slice in half. Place in a dish and add the remaining ingredients. Cook in the microwave for 5 minutes, stopping halfway to rearrange the fruit (so that the bananas in the centre are moved to the outside of the dish and vice versa). Serve hot with cream.

Variations

Rum bananas: Substitute rum for the wine in the above recipe.
Walnut banana bake: Add 50 g/2 oz chopped walnuts to the bananas.

VANILLA ICE CREAM

SERVES 4

2 eggs, whisked
450 ml/$\frac{3}{4}$ pint milk
175 g/6 oz caster sugar
1 tablespoon vanilla essence
300 ml/$\frac{1}{2}$ pint double cream

Combine the eggs, milk and sugar in a basin or mixing bowl and cook in the microwave for 6 minutes, stirring frequently. Allow to cool, then stir in the vanilla essence and cream. Pour into a freezing tray or a rigid shallow plastic container and freeze until semi-solid. Whisk again and return to the freezer. Allow to stand at room temperature for 1–2 hours before serving.

Clockwise from top left: Grapefruit Cheesecake (overleaf), Crunchy Apple Crisp (page 68), Pineapple and Orange Turnabout (page 68) and Banana Bake

GRAPEFRUIT CHEESECAKE
SERVES 4–6

50 g/2 oz butter
125 g/4 oz digestive biscuits, crushed
175 g/6 oz cream cheese
2 eggs, lightly whisked
pinch salt
75 g/3 oz caster sugar
3 tablespoons undiluted grapefruit
juice, thawed
vanilla essence to taste
almond essence to taste
100 ml/4 fl oz soured cream
Decoration:
150 ml/¼ pint double cream, whipped
grapefruit segments

Place the butter in a basin and melt in the microwave for 30 seconds. Stir in the crushed biscuit crumbs and mix well. Press into a flan dish, lining the base and sides evenly.

Lightly whisk the remaining ingredients together until well blended and smooth. Pour into the flan dish and cook in the microwave for 2 minutes, turning the dish after 1 minute. Cook in the microwave for a further minute, turning after 30 seconds. Allow to stand for 1 minute, then return to the microwave for 1 minute, turning after 30 seconds. Allow to cool, then chill in the refrigerator.

Decorate with whipped cream and grapefruit segments.

Variation
Use undiluted orange juice in place of the grapefruit juice.

CRÈME CARAMEL
SERVES 4

Caramel:
6 tablespoons caster sugar
3 tablespoons hand-hot
water (about 48 C/120 F)
Custard:
2 eggs
1½ tablespoons caster sugar
450 ml/¾ pint milk

Mix together the sugar and water in a pudding basin and cook in the microwave for approximately 8 minutes or until the caramel turns a dark golden colour. If uneven browning occurs it may be necessary to stir the caramel once during cooking. Coat the base and insides of each ramekin with the caramel and set aside to cool.

Lightly whisk together the eggs and sugar for the custard and stir in the milk. Pour the custard into the ramekin dishes and place them in an oblong dish. Pour almost boiling water in the dish to surround the ramekins up to the level of the custard. Cook in the microwave for 8½ minutes, turning the large dish and ramekin dishes 3–4 times during cooking, until the custards are lightly set – they will become more firm on chilling.

Place the custards in a refrigerator to chill, preferably overnight. When required, turn out and serve with whipped cream.

CARAMELISED ORANGES

SERVES 4

4 large oranges
175 g/6 oz caster sugar
100 ml/4 fl oz cold water
150 ml/¼ pint double cream
1 tablespoon Grand Marnier

Pare a thin piece of rind off one of the oranges. Cut this into fine shreds and place these in a bowl of iced water; they will be used as decoration.

Peel the oranges and remove all the pith. Slice the oranges, remove any pith from the centre and all the pips. Place the slices back together to re-form the orange shape or, alternatively, arrange the slices in a suitable serving dish which will withstand the heat of the caramel.

Place the sugar and water in a pudding basin and cook in the microwave for approximately 12 minutes until it becomes a dark golden colour. The caramel may need stirring once or twice during cooking if uneven caramelisation occurs, but this should be avoided if possible. Drain the strips of

Caramelised Oranges

orange rind and sprinkle them over the fruit. Pour the caramel over the oranges.

Allow the oranges to cool, then chill them overnight in the refrigerator and serve with the cream whipped with the Grand Marnier.

PEARS IN WINE

SERVES 4

4 ripe even-sized pears
600 ml/1 pint red wine
pinch nutmeg
1 (5-cm/2-inch) stick cinnamon
50 g/2 oz sugar
pared rind of ½ lemon
few drops lemon juice
4 cloves

Peel the pears, leaving whole with the stalks on. Place the remaining ingredients in a dish or bowl and cook in the microwave for 5 minutes. Carefully place the pears in the hot wine and return to the microwave for a further 5 minutes. Leave to stand for 5 minutes before serving.

Menus

When cooking a complete meal in the microwave oven, timing needs to be very carefully planned, to allow the dishes to be separately cooked, yet still be piping hot and ready to eat when required.

BREAKFAST FOR 1

*2 rashers streaky bacon
2 chippolata sausages
1 egg
1 tomato*

Wrap the bacon rashers around the sausages and place on the plate. Butter a ramekin dish, break in the egg and stand on the plate. Add the halved tomato. Cook in the microwave for 2 minutes, turning the dish once.

Note: Cooking for 2 minutes produces an egg with a slightly soft yolk. If a very soft egg is required, the ramekin dish should be placed on the plate after 30 seconds cooking time.

COMPLETE BREAKFAST FOR 1

Total microwave cooking time = 4¼ minutes

Sausage, egg, tomato and bacon
(see above – 2 minutes)
Roll and butter
reheat roll – 15 seconds
Coffee
heat coffee – 2 minutes

Advance preparation
Place all the food on a plate and cover, either the previous night or just before cooking.
Note: If the food has been refrigerated overnight the microwave cooking time will need to be increased.

When required
Cook the food on the plate in the microwave. Heat the roll and then the coffee in the microwave.

LUNCHEON FOR 4

Total microwave cooking time = 24 minutes

Paella
(see page 65) – 19 minutes
Green salad
Banana bake
(see page 70) – 5 minutes

Advance preparation
Prepare and assemble the salad.
Prepare ingredients for the paella.
Make and assemble for Banana bake.

When guests arrive
Cook paella in the microwave.
Whilst eating the main course cook the Banana in the microwave and leave to stand before serving.

DINNER PARTY FOR 4

Total microwave cooking time = 56 minutes

Grapefruit with vermouth
(see page 24) – 2 minutes
Rolled galantine of chicken
(see page 33) 20 minutes
New potatoes
(see chart page 46–47) – 10 minutes
Courgettes
(see chart page 46–47) – 3 minutes
Crème caramel
(see page 72) – 16½ minutes
Coffee
reheat ready-made – 4½ minutes

Advance preparation
Prepare and cook the Crème caramel the previous day and chill overnight
Bone and stuff the chicken.
Prepare the grapefruit.
Prepare the vegetables for the Lyonnaise potatoes and cook the onions in the microwave. Arrange the onions and potatoes in layers in the dish.

When guests arrive
Cook the stuffed chicken in the microwave and stand for 15 minutes.
Whilst the chicken is standing . . . pour the cream over the potatoes and cook in the microwave for 5 minutes, remove and allow to stand whilst cooking the grapefruit.
Return the potatoes to the microwave and continue with the cooking time.
Serve the grapefruit.
Remove the potatoes from the microwave and cook the courgettes whilst slicing the chicken.
Heat the coffee in the microwave.

Index